WHEN OUR HATS DON'T MATCH

WHY FAMILIAR PEOPLE FEEL DISTANT, AND HOW TO FIND THEM AGAIN

KUSHAL STHAPAK

Made with ♥ on the Notion Press Platform
www.notionpress.com

*To the quiet companions of our lives—
those we misread, mistimed, or mistook for distant,
only to later realize they were simply overwhelmed
by the weight of too many hats.*

*To every parent—who carried entire worlds on their shoulders,
wore their roles like second skin,
and asked for nothing but gave everything.*

*To the siblings, cousins, friends, and family
who became the background music of our days—
rarely centre stage, yet always composing
the quiet symphony of love, effort, and presence.*

*To you—
if you've ever taken silence too personally,
if you've ever questioned why someone you loved felt far away,
or doubted your own place in their life—
this book is written so you'd know:
it wasn't you.
It was just the hats.*

*And to every soul who ever wondered
why a familiar face felt far away—
may you find your anchor again,
and may it lead you home.*

This book is for you.

Contents

When Our Hats Don't Match

"Most bonds don't end in arguments.

They erode in misunderstood silences."

- Kushal Sthapak

Preface

I have always noticed people judging others or speaking about them in various ways—sometimes warmly, sometimes harshly, and often inconsistently. The same person can be praised one day and criticized the next, depending on the situation or the mood of the person talking about them. Over time, observing countless such conversations and reflecting on my own experiences, I began to see a pattern.

Through the teachings I've received from my parents, family, and life itself, I've realized that much of how we perceive others is filtered through the momentary hats they wear—roles, obligations, moods, and responsibilities. What if, instead of reacting to someone's temporary behavior, we looked deeper into who they are at their core? What if we stopped judging based on fleeting actions and instead anchored ourselves to the part of them that remains consistent?

This book was born out of a desire to help others see that perspective. To help people zoom out from daily noise and misunderstandings, and reconnect with others by understanding the deeper, truer version of them. Because when we understand that part—the part that rarely changes—we begin to live with more compassion, less judgment, and greater peace.

Prologue

It's your last day at work.

You've been wrapping up projects, clearing your desk, handing over notes. You're ready to leave—but not ready for what the day has in store.

The team has planned a farewell. There are cupcakes, laughter, a few handmade posters on the wall, and a slideshow of blurry pictures from office off-sites. Someone has even dug up your first email thread and is reading it aloud, badly impersonating your tone.

Your usually reserved manager says something thoughtful. The intern you mentored leaves a card with words that hit deeper than expected. People share stories about you—small, strange, wonderful stories. About your coffee preferences. About the way you once saved a client call. About how you remembered everyone's birthdays.

And for a few hours, you are at the center of everyone's world.

You feel it. That rare feeling of being completely seen. Fully appreciated. Not for your KPIs or deadlines—but for the person you've been in that space.

Then the day ends.

A few days pass.

You check your phone out of habit, expecting something from someone—just a "how's it going?" or an inside joke. Nothing. The group chat goes quiet. No more pings. No more "hey, remember when..."

People move on. You do too.

But something lingers. You wonder: *Did they really care? Or was it just part of the script? A moment of politeness dressed up as meaning?*

You didn't imagine it.

They didn't fake it.

And no, nothing changed.

In that moment, when they were fully present for you, they wore just one hat—the one they wore for *you*. Not as a manager, or a colleague, or a team lead juggling deadlines. Just someone showing up for someone else. That moment was real. That version of them was real.

What came after—silence, distance, absence—was real too. But it didn't cancel what came before.

This book is about that space.
The space between connection and confusion.
Between feeling seen and suddenly unseen.
Between the version of someone you hold close—and the one who seems to drift away.

It's not about fixing people.
It's about seeing them—clearly.

And sometimes, in seeing others clearly, we begin to see ourselves too.

CHAPTER ONE

THE DISAPPEARING VILLAGE

*"We didn't grow apart; we simply grew into lives
that no longer spoke the same language."*

There was a time when life felt... stitched together. Not by devices or calendars, but by people—warm, present, familiar.

You probably remember it. Summer holidays in your childhood. Visiting your grandparents' home. A single house somehow hosting three generations—noisy laughter, overlapping conversations, clanging plates, and at least five people who claimed they "raised you more than your parents ever did."

You weren't alone then. You couldn't be. Even if you tried to sneak away, someone would catch you—either with a question, a task, or a story that pulled you back into the fold.

There was something so natural about that rhythm. You knew your cousins. Not just their names or Instagram handles—but their habits, their moods, the way they rolled their eyes when scolded. You had seen them cry, fight, sneak food from the kitchen, get jealous of new toys. You knew them. And they knew you.

It didn't matter that some relatives lived in cities far away. They always returned—every summer, every Diwali, every major family event. They came home. That's what people did.

Back then, nobody had to "schedule a call." Conversations just happened. Nobody had to "make time." Time made itself.

Now, that village is disappearing.

We still love the people. We still care. But somehow, we don't know them anymore.

Our cousins are strangers in nice clothes at weddings. Our friends are always "busy but let's catch up soon." Our neighbors are behind doors we never knock on. And we're all somewhere in the middle—missing people without knowing what to do about it.

It's not just nostalgia. It's a fracture.

Let me tell you about Sahil.

Sahil grew up in a joint family in Lucknow—fifteen people under one roof. His cousins were like siblings. His happiest memories were nights when everyone would gather around their grandfather's old transistor and end up singing songs over chai and mango slices.

He remembers how the back veranda would fill up with charpais during power cuts, and how everyone—children, adults, grandparents—would sleep outside under the stars, fighting over who gets the corner spot, laughing at ghost stories.

Now Sahil lives in Bangalore, in a 1BHK with white walls and good

Wi-Fi. He has a stable job, a gym membership, and a dozen group chats that are muted.

When he visits home, it's not the same. The house feels quieter. His cousins come at different times. Some are married, some are abroad. They talk, yes—but mostly about traffic, work stress, or where to invest next.

Once, Sahil asked one of his closest cousins to go out for a walk—just like old times. She smiled and said she was tired. "Maybe next time."

There was no next time.

And Sahil realized, quietly, that the village he once lived in now only existed in memory.

Let me tell you another story.

Tanya used to walk to school every day with her neighbor, Priya. They weren't best friends, but they shared that comforting familiarity—sharing snacks, complaining about homework, and once even getting scolded together for drawing cartoons on the classroom blackboard.

Priya was the kind of person who always noticed if Tanya wore new shoes or had a band-aid on her finger. And Tanya always waited for Priya before entering class, even if it meant being late by a minute.

Years later, Tanya saw Priya at a wedding. Same face, slightly different smile. They hugged politely. Exchanged some updates. Said "we should definitely meet up soon." They never did.

And that's the thing.

Sometimes people don't leave with drama or fights. They just... fade.

Into routines. Into new cities. Into newer connections. Or sometimes just into a different version of themselves.

And when you meet them again, they're kind, they're warm, but they're not yours anymore. Not in the way they once were.

Now let me introduce one more person—Shivansh.

Shivansh lives in a small apartment in Pune. Every morning, he steps out and nods at his neighbor, Mr. Deshmukh, who used to be his tea partner every Sunday morning during the lockdown.

They would sit by the apartment staircase, sipping tea, sharing thoughts about life, family, and everything in between. Shivansh once told Deshmukh about his failed engagement. Deshmukh once shared stories of his son's struggles abroad.

Now, two years later, they barely wave at each other.

Not because anything happened. Nothing did.

Life just picked up speed again. Sunday mornings got replaced by work emails, errands, grocery runs, and scrolling feeds.

The connection didn't end. It just quietly went to sleep.

So what happened?

Is it the Western influence? The shrinking family structures? The glorification of "personal space"? Sure, all of it plays a part.

But there's something deeper too.

We've stopped seeing people fully. We interact with fragments—their latest update, their professional identity, their mood that day. We've forgotten that everyone around us is a complex, layered human being—just like us.

And in forgetting, we lose the thread. The one that connects who we were with who we are.

The village didn't disappear in one day. It faded.
Through busyness. Through assumptions. Through moments when we could've reached out and didn't.

But what if we could find it again? Not by going back. But by learning to see the people around us with new eyes. To understand them not just by what they say or do, but by what might be happening behind their silence. To interpret their behavior with softness instead of suspicion. To recognize that what we receive from someone in a given moment isn't always the sum of who they are—but often a snapshot filtered by the hats they're wearing that day.

And that's where this book begins.
With an invitation.
To see people more clearly.
To hold onto the version of them that once felt whole—and to trust that it still exists, even when it's buried under layers of noise and responsibility.

Let me tell you one last story. Let me share another story that might feel familiar.

Neha works in Gurgaon, and her job demands everything—long hours, sharp deadlines, late-night meetings with teams across time zones. Her college roommate, Aditi, lives just 25 minutes away. They used to be inseparable—sharing meals, midnight walks, heartbreaks, and dreams of the future.

Now, they only see each other on birthdays, and even that feels rushed.

Last time they met, Aditi brought a handmade photo frame with a picture of their old hostel room. Neha smiled, touched. But also, strangely awkward.

There was love in the room. But also distance. And neither knew how to bridge it.

Neha often thinks of calling Aditi randomly—just to talk. But every time she gets a breather from work, she ends up scrolling reels instead.

Aditi, on the other hand, doesn't want to disturb Neha during her work hours. And so, both wait.

And in that waiting, they drift further.

But that love? It's still there.

It's just lying beneath the weight of schedules, assumptions, and the fear of being too late. This is the world we now live in.
People care, but they don't know how to show it anymore.
We all carry love like unread messages—meant to be sent, but stuck in drafts.

And that's why it's not enough to just "reconnect."
We must re-learn how to see the people we already have.
Because when we stop misreading them, we might find that the love was never lost. Just misplaced.
Let me take you back to Diwali, a few years ago.

For years, your family had the same rhythm: light diyas together, make rangolis with cousins, and wait for the homemade sweets from that one aunt who always went overboard in the best way. Even the arguments had their own tradition—someone would complain about the noise, someone else would scold kids for wasting crackers, and the family would laugh over it all by dessert.

But this year, things were... quieter.

Some relatives didn't come. Others came, but left early. There were more phones than people at the dinner table. Your cousin, the one you used to fight over sparklers with, sat in a corner replying to work emails. That one uncle who never missed a celebration? Joined over a video call. Five minutes.

You smiled, you celebrated—but something felt missing.

That something wasn't the food or the lights or the gifts. It was the thread. The invisible thread that once ran through every person in the house and tied everyone together like fairy lights across a balcony.

And when that thread begins to loosen, the lights still shine—but not quite the same way.
But here's the thing: the thread isn't gone.
It's just waiting.

Waiting for someone to notice. To tug at it gently. To remind everyone that it still exists—and can still be rewoven.

And maybe that someone is you.

This book isn't about going back in time.
It's about noticing the time we're in—and choosing, deliberately, to reconnect.

Not with all, maybe. But with a few.
Not every day. But sometimes.
Not through grand gestures. But through honest, human ones.

Because the village may be fading, yes.
But your place in it doesn't have to.

Pause and Reflect

- Who are the people you once felt deeply connected to—but now only see occasionally?

- Can you remember a version of them that felt completely present, joyful, and true?

- What if that version still exists—just hidden beneath the layers of life?

- Are there ways you can let them know you're still holding that version of them—without asking them to prove it again?

- Is there a family ritual or moment that used to bring everyone together?

- What changed? Was it time, distance, or just unspoken assumptions?

- What if rekindling even one of those old rhythms could help bring a piece of the village back?

Villages don't disappear all at once. They fade in missed calls, postponed plans, and the silence between words. But somewhere beneath it all, the warmth still lingers—waiting for one person to light the lamp, so others can find their way back home.

The village isn't lost—it's simply waiting to be remembered.

CHAPTER TWO

THE MANY HATS WE WEAR

*"We clash not with people, but with
the hats they are forced to wear."*

Do you remember the last time someone surprised you—not with a gift or a party, but with their behavior

Maybe a friend didn't return your calls when you needed them most. Or a colleague who was always calm suddenly snapped at you. Or a cousin you always considered self-centered went out of their way to help you during a family emergency.

Each of these moments leaves us with a sense of confusion. What happened to the person we thought we knew?

Let's begin here.

Rajeshwari was hosting a small reunion at her home in Pune. Six old college friends. She cooked, cleaned, and spent days imagining how it would feel to have everyone under one roof again.

Everyone showed up, except Anu.

Anu sent a message: "Hey, stuck with something. Hope it goes well!" No call. No apology. No explanation.

The evening was lovely, but Rajeshwari kept wondering why Anu—her closest college friend—would skip without a proper reason. Over the next few days, she kept replaying old conversations. Had she said something wrong? Was Anu upset?

Weeks later, she found out that Anu had been helping her brother, who had just returned from rehab. He had relapsed, and the family was going through a storm.

Rajeshwari felt a strange mix of guilt and understanding. Not because she had judged Anu—but because she had forgotten that people live entire lives outside of their relationship with us.

And that's where the idea of "hats" begins.

We all wear multiple hats—sometimes in a single day, sometimes all at once. A hat for the role of a parent, one for a sibling, another for a team lead, one for a friend, one for a caregiver, and sometimes one just to hold ourselves together.

Every interaction you have with someone is colored by the hat they're wearing in that moment. And depending on which hat is louder, more urgent, or heavier, their behavior may change.

Let's say you message a friend and they reply with just a "hmm." If they're wearing the hat of a worried parent dealing with a sick child, or an employee under pressure from a deadline, that message makes sense. It's not about you. It's about the hat.

But in our minds, we often forget the hats. We take every

interaction at face value, as if it represents the whole person.

Now imagine someone in your life. Your best friend. Your partner. Your sibling.

In your head, they occupy a specific identity—that of *your* person. Someone who is supposed to act a certain way, respond in specific patterns, and behave in a manner that aligns with your emotional blueprint for them.

But the truth is, they're also someone else's person. Someone's boss. Someone's child. Someone's dependent. And all these roles coexist, often colliding, rarely aligning perfectly.

Let's take Harshit's story.

Harshit is a father of a 3-year-old. He's also the only son of an aging father. At work, he leads a product team of twenty people. And in between, he's also trying to be a decent husband, an attentive friend, and a responsible adult who hasn't yet figured out how to file his taxes without stress.

His friend Kunal, who lives in another city, calls him once every couple of weeks. Sometimes Harshit picks up immediately. Other times, he misses the call and forgets to call back.

Last month, Kunal sent a short text: "Bro, you've changed. Let me know if you still want to stay in touch."

That message hurt. Not because it was cruel. But because it didn't see the hats.

Kunal was expecting a response from Harshit, the friend. But the version of Harshit who received the call that day was also balancing a toddler with a fever, a work deadline, and a father asking him to help install a ceiling fan.

Which version should have picked up?

This isn't to excuse behavior. It's not to say people never neglect or avoid. But it is to say that human behavior is not always personal—even when it feels that way.

Let me take you into another everyday moment.

Shivani and Shagun work in the same office. They're not close friends but have shared many coffee breaks. Shivani recently lost her pet, something that left her devastated. At work, she didn't want to talk about it. She buried herself in emails and headphones.

Shagun noticed. But when she asked, Shivani brushed it off with a tight smile and a "just tired."

A few days later, Shagun heard from someone else about the pet.

She felt guilty. Why didn't she ask again? Was she too quick to assume Shivani was being cold?

And that's the question, isn't it? How often do we let one expression, one silence, one missed response define our entire perception of someone?

The problem isn't that people change. The problem is that we expect them not to. We expect them to freeze in the role we've assigned them.

But life doesn't work that way.

Every person is a walking collage of identities, priorities, and pressures. And in any given moment, the hat they're wearing may not be the one you need them to wear.

So what do we do with this knowledge?

We learn to interpret with grace.

When someone doesn't show up the way you expected them to, ask yourself: What hat might they be wearing right now?

When someone surprises you with kindness you didn't think they were capable of, ask: What hat allowed that version to emerge?

Understanding people means understanding that you don't always get their whole self—just the part that is available to you, shaped by what they're carrying.

And you? You wear hats too.

There are days when you want to be the loyal friend but end up being the distracted employee. Days when you want to listen patiently but find yourself snapping because your patience was already used up in another hat you wore earlier that day.

You are not one-dimensional. Neither is anyone else.

Let's pause here.

This doesn't mean we stop expecting people to be present or kind or consistent. But it does mean we offer them a little more room to be human.

And here's something important: we'll be diving deeper into the idea of hats in Chapter 5. That's where we unpack what it means to wear a single hat in an extreme moment—and how that reveals a person's truest self. So for now, consider this chapter a gentle doorway into that idea.

Let's bridge back to Chapter 1 for a moment.

Remember the disappearing village? That space of warmth, attention, and easy togetherness?

What kept the village alive wasn't just proximity. It was familiarity with the hats. You saw your cousin being a troublemaker with his siblings and a helper to the elders. You saw your aunt being stern one moment and soft the next. You saw the full range.

So you didn't judge them by one hat. You knew they wore many.

Now, in the isolated spaces of modern life, we often see people in fragments. One version. One lens. One role.

And that makes misunderstanding easy. That makes judgment quicker. That makes distance grow.

The next time you feel someone has pulled away, changed, or disappointed you—pause. Breathe. Wonder, just for a second: What hat are they wearing today?

It might not match yours. And that's okay.

Because the more we see the hats, the more we begin to see the person beneath them.

Pause and Reflect

- Think of someone who's been behaving differently with you lately. Can you guess what hats they might be wearing?

- Has someone misunderstood you recently? Which of your hats were they unable to see?

- Is there a version of someone you miss—a side of them you haven't seen in a while? Could it be waiting beneath a louder, heavier hat?

Next time you speak to someone you care about, try this: don't just ask how they are. Ask what they're holding.

It might just show you a whole new version of someone you thought you knew.

CHAPTER THREE

FAMILIAR STRANGERS

*"Familiarity fades not with time, but with
the weight of new hats we never got to know."*

It's strange, isn't it? How someone can be in your life for years, and yet feel unfamiliar.

You share a meal. You exchange wishes on birthdays. You ask about work, about health, about the kids.

But you walk away feeling like you spoke to a shadow. The real person, it seems, was missing.

Let me take you back to a quiet Sunday morning in Jaipur.

Shailja was visiting her parents after months. Her father's cousin, Arun Uncle, was also visiting—a man Shailja had seen countless times growing up. He was always there at family weddings, birthdays, and other milestone celebrations. He would tell jokes, bring sweets, and tease Shailja about how tall she'd grown.

But that morning, something shifted.

They were both sitting on the terrace, sipping chai.

Shailja asked him, casually, "Uncle, you're always traveling. Don't you ever get tired?"

He laughed. But then he said something unexpected: "Tired, yes. But when I'm home, nobody asks me how I feel. When I'm on the move, I'm needed."

Shailja looked at him—really looked. And for the first time, she saw not her uncle, not the funny family man with anecdotes, but someone quietly aching to matter.

She hadn't seen that version before. Or maybe she had just never looked for it.

This is what happens with familiar people.

We see them so often that we stop seeing them at all.

We assign them roles—mother, friend, neighbor, cousin. And with that role, we attach expectations, assumptions, and a preset script.

We stop being curious. We start operating on autopilot.

Remember Renu, the school librarian?

She was quiet, efficient, and always wrapped books in brown covers like they were something sacred.

Most students saw her as strict. Never smiling. Always policing noise.

Until one day, Ayush, a ninth grader, forgot his lunch. His stomach growled so loudly in the reading room that even the encyclopedias looked concerned.

Renu called him to her desk. Without a word, she pulled out a neatly packed roti roll from her tiffin and handed it over. Then she told him, "Come to me if this happens again. Don't sit hungry."

That moment spread quietly across the school. Suddenly, students saw her differently. Not just as a librarian, but as someone who noticed, who cared, who remembered what it felt like to be overlooked.

How many Renu-like people surround us?

How many do we misread simply because we've locked them into a narrow definition?

This chapter is about unlocking those definitions.

Because here's the truth: The closer someone is, the easier it is to misread them.

Why?

Because familiarity breeds patterns. And patterns, while comforting, can be deceiving.

You assume your elder brother is indifferent because he never says "I love you." But maybe he checks your car every time you visit because that's how he says it.
You assume your cousin is self-absorbed because she always talks about her job. But maybe it's the only part of her life that makes her feel accomplished.

You assume your friend is becoming distant because she replies late. But maybe she's overwhelmed, and the one message she does send is her way of holding on.

We misread love, care, anxiety, and affection—just because they don't arrive in the format we prefer.

Let's bring in another story.

Neeraj and Karthik had been friends since college. They once shared everything—from vada pavs to heartbreaks. But over the years, their conversations thinned.

Karthik moved to another city. Neeraj got busy with work. And gradually, the calls turned into texts, then forwards, then silence.

One day, Neeraj's mother fell seriously ill. The first person who showed up at the hospital was Karthik. Not with flowers. Not with grand words. But with a flask of filter coffee and a file containing all the hospital paperwork.

"You always forget forms," he said. "So I called ahead."

Neeraj smiled, eyes misty. That one gesture said what months of silence couldn't.

People don't always say what they feel. But they often show it—in ways that don't match our expectations.

That's the risk of reading people only through our lens.

We don't see their hat—we see our own.

Yes, we mentioned hats earlier. And we'll talk more deeply about that in Chapter 5. But this chapter is where we begin to understand the gap those hats create.

Your hat might say, "I need affection right now."

Their hat might say, "I'm barely staying afloat today."

And if we're not careful, that mismatch can feel like rejection.

But often, it's not rejection. It's just misalignment.

Imagine you're tuning a radio. You're both on the same frequency band, just slightly off. All you hear is static. But a small shift can bring back the music.

To do that, you must tune. You must pause. You must choose curiosity over assumption.

So how do we do that?

One way is to listen for the unsaid.

If someone always jokes but never shares, ask what they're hiding behind the humor.

If someone seems fine but cancels plans often, ask what their silence is trying to manage.

Another way is to revisit the past.

Recall moments where someone showed up for you in ways you hadn't noticed then. A lift to the station. A reminder to eat. A hand on your shoulder when words failed.

Those were their ways of saying, "I see you. I'm here."

We don't lose people all at once. We lose them in moments of misreading, in unspoken frustrations, in the slow erosion of curiosity.

But we can find them again.

Not by asking them to change. But by changing the way we look at them.

Not by waiting for them to meet our needs. But by meeting them where they are.

In the small, often unnoticed gestures, lies the real map to reconnection.

The tea someone makes without asking. The message that simply says, "reached home?" The forward that reminds you of a shared memory. The silence that trusts you to understand.

These are not gaps. They are bridges. We just need to walk across.

Pause and Reflect

- Who is someone you see often but feel distant from?

- Are you interpreting their behavior through your needs, or trying to understand theirs?

- What if the version you miss is still there—just speaking a different language of connection?

This chapter is a gentle reminder:

Familiarity isn't the same as understanding.

The people closest to us can still surprise us, heal us, and break through our assumptions—if we let them.

All it takes is a little curiosity. A little grace. And the willingness to see them again, as if for the first time.

CHAPTER FOUR

LOST IN TRANSLATION

"In the space between what is spoken and what is heard,
entire worlds are born and broken."

Have you ever been in a conversation where you walked away thinking, "That's not what I meant," or "Why did they take it that way?"

We speak, they hear. But somehow, what is heard is not always what was said.

Let me begin with a story.

Karan and Ishita had been married for eight years. One Sunday morning, over breakfast, Karan casually said, "We should start eating healthier."

He meant it neutrally. A suggestion, born from his recent obsession with YouTube fitness videos.

But Ishita went silent.

Later, she said, "I get it. I'm not slim enough for you anymore."

Karan was stunned. "That's not what I said."

"But that's what I heard," she replied.

This happens more often than we admit.

Because between what is said and what is heard lies a space filled with our assumptions, our insecurities, our past experiences, and the hats we are wearing in that moment.

When Karan spoke, he was wearing the hat of a health enthusiast, excited about smoothies and step goals. But Ishita heard it wearing the hat of a woman already feeling under pressure from society's beauty standards.

Same words. Two different hats. Two completely different interpretations.

That's what this chapter is about.

So many of our misunderstandings are not rooted in intention, but in translation.

Think about your workplace.

Your manager says, "Can you send me that report by today?"

You might hear urgency, pressure, or even mistrust.

But maybe your manager is wearing the hat of someone just trying to wrap up their day early. No subtext. Just a task.

Or your friend says, "You never call anymore."

You might hear blame. But maybe, behind their words, is a quiet longing: "I miss you."

Words are rarely just words. They carry emotions, histories, and unspoken needs. And they often get tangled in the noise of our expectations.

Let's bring in another story.

Vaishnavi had recently moved to Delhi for a new job. She called her mother, excited to share that she'd cooked rajma chawal all by herself.

Her mother replied, "That's good. But don't forget to use less salt. You always overdo it."

Vaishnavi smiled on the phone but felt deflated. What was meant to be a proud moment turned sour.

Two days later, she visited home.

That evening, her mother served rajma.

"This tastes exactly like the one I make," Vaishnavi said.

"It is yours," her mother replied. "I had some left from your visit. I froze it."

Vaishnavi was stunned.

"Why didn't you say anything when I called?" she asked.

Her mother simply said, "I was just... being your mother."

Sometimes, love wears the hat of correction. Of advice. Of worry. It doesn't always sound like celebration, but the feeling is still love.

And unless we listen carefully, we miss it.

We interpret the correction as criticism. The silence as disinterest. The reminder as nagging.

But behind these moments often lies care, protection, and deep affection—just wearing an imperfect hat.

You might remember from Chapter 2 that everyone wears multiple hats. And we promised to explore the meaning of those hats more deeply in Chapter 5. But here's where the idea starts to really touch our everyday life.

Because when someone wears a hat, it affects not only how they behave but also how they speak—and how they listen.

When you talk to someone wearing the hat of a professional under pressure, they may hear urgency in your casual tone.

When you talk to someone wearing the hat of a caregiver, they may respond with caution, always thinking ten steps ahead.

Even your words of appreciation might sound like pity to someone wearing the hat of low self-worth.

That's why so many of our conversations feel like missed connections.

We're not speaking different languages. But we're living in different interpretations.

And here's the strange part: even when we know someone well, these disconnects can still happen.

Especially then.

Because we assume they should understand us better. And when they don't, the hurt feels sharper.

But maybe, instead of assuming, we pause. We ask, "What hat are they wearing right now?"

Because when we see the hat, we understand the tone.

When we understand the tone, we forgive the words.

Let's take a short second example.

Ira and Sonali worked together at a startup. Ira had just been promoted, a well-deserved milestone after months of relentless effort. She walked into the office with quiet pride, expecting a few warm congratulations from her peers.

Sonali, usually reserved, looked up from her desk and said flatly, "Well, enjoy it while it lasts."

The words cut deeper than they should have.

Ira was confused. Hurt. They had worked side by side for years.

Later that evening, while leaving office, Sonali hesitated before speaking.

"I was in the final round too," she said. "And honestly... I thought it would be me."

There it was.

Sonali wasn't being spiteful. She was being human—wearing the hat of disappointment, of bruised expectations.

Understanding that didn't erase the sting Ira felt. But it softened it. And in that softness, empathy made space for healing.

That's what understanding does. It doesn't always excuse the behavior. But it explains it.

And sometimes, that's enough.

Can you think of a conversation that didn't go the way you wanted? What hat were you wearing? What hat might they have been wearing?

Is there someone you need to hear again, but with fresh ears?

What would change if we stopped assuming intention and started exploring interpretation?

We don't need perfect words. We need a willingness to see the human underneath them.

Every conversation is an opportunity. To connect. To clarify. To bridge.

Let's not lose each other in translation.

Pause and Reflect

- Think of a recent conversation that left you unsettled. What did you mean to say? What might the other person have heard?

- What hat were you wearing in that moment? And what hat might they have been wearing?

- Has there been a time when someone misunderstood your intentions? How would the outcome have changed if they had seen the hat you were wearing?

- Are there relationships in your life where repeated miscommunications have built silent walls?

- Can you revisit those moments with a different lens—not to change what was said, but to understand what was heard?

Sometimes, healing doesn't require the perfect apology—just a clearer understanding of what truly unfolded between two people wearing different hats.

CHAPTER FIVE

THE ONE TRUE HAT

*"Amid the noise of borrowed identities, the real self emerges,
silent yet resonant, fleeting yet unforgettable."*

Some chapters in life whisper. Others arrive with a sudden clarity—a kind of silence that says, "Now you see it."

This is that chapter.

Let's go back for a moment.

In the very first chapter, we remembered a simpler time—the disappearing village of family gatherings, handwritten letters, and the warmth of being truly known.

Then, we spoke of masks, roles, and the many hats people wear. We tried to understand what goes wrong when communication falters, when love gets misheard, and when intentions vanish in translation.

All of it has been leading up to this.

The moment we realize: what we often judge as someone's personality is simply the hat they are wearing in that moment.

But what if, every once in a while, we get to see someone wearing only one hat—the one meant just for us?

Let me tell you a story.

Shubham had just gotten married. It was a grand yet intimate celebration in a quaint town near Udaipur, nestled amidst hills and mustard fields. The kind of wedding where lanterns lined the courtyard, the scent of mogra filled the air, and laughter echoed through old haveli walls.

His entire family had gathered—relatives who hadn't spoken in years found themselves sharing a plate of jalebi. Friends flew in from different cities. His college roommate DJed the sangeet night. His aunt, who never danced at any function, broke into a full-on Bollywood number. Even the cousin who rarely expressed emotions cried during the vidaai.

Uncles reminisced about Shubham's childhood mishaps. Neighbors pitched in to help with decorations. Children ran around carrying trays and misplacing gifts. It was chaos, but it was beautiful.

For three full days, Shubham wasn't just a groom—he was everyone's person. Every guest, every relative, every friend—wore just one hat: Shubham's person. Their attention, energy, love—all directed at him.

Shubham later told his wife, "I never knew everyone loved me this much."

But a few months after the wedding, that feeling began to fade.

He texted his favorite cousin. No reply.

He messaged the same aunt who had danced at his sangeet—she

read but didn't respond.

He tried to plan a get-together with his old friends, but no one had the time.

It hurt.

That's when his wife said something that stayed with him: "They didn't change. It's just that, for those three days, you were the only hat they wore. Now, they've gone back to wearing others too."

It clicked.

That same cousin was now a new father. His aunt was caring for her aging mother-in-law. His friends were immersed in jobs, deadlines, and navigating early parenthood.

But in those wedding days, they had paused their lives. They had set aside the hats of professionals, caregivers, partners, and more. They wore only one hat— Shubham's person. And when they did, their best selves showed up.

That was the truth of who they could be.

And that's the hat this chapter is about.

The one true hat.

The one people wear when everything else is stripped away—when they are simply your friend, sibling, child, neighbor. Nothing more, nothing less.

We don't get to see this hat often. Life rarely gives people the space to wear just one. They're juggling deadlines, identities, responsibilities.

But when we do see it—even once—it is enough.

Because that moment? That's who they really are, when all the noise fades.

If you think back to your own life, you'll notice something:

Your friend who stood by your side during your stressful job change.

Your cousin who danced with you like a fool at your wedding, leaving his own worries behind.

Your neighbor who surprised you with tea and snacks after a long day because they just "had a feeling."

In those moments, they weren't balancing roles. They weren't distracted. They showed up as just your person.

That's the hat.

And that version of them—it might be rare, but it's real.

So what if, instead of judging people by how they behave on a random Tuesday, we judged them by how they show up when they wear that one hat?

What if we gave more weight to that version of them, than to the version that didn't text us back?

Wouldn't our relationships feel fuller? Kinder? More forgiving?

Here's another story.

Ishaan and Rhea were close friends from college. They used to talk every other day. But ever since Rhea moved to a new city, things got quiet. Fewer texts. Fewer calls. Life had gotten busy for both of them.

Then came a big day—Rhea was showcasing her first solo art gallery. She had worked day and night for months.

She had invited a handful of close people. Most sent good-luck messages. But Ishaan didn't even respond.

The day of the event, just an hour before it began, as Rhea was setting up her pieces and pacing nervously, Ishaan walked in.

No fanfare. Just a bag of her favorite snacks and a quiet smile.

"I didn't text because I was figuring out a way to be here," he said.

He had taken an overnight bus. Canceled meetings. Rearranged everything. Just to wear one hat that day—the one that said, "I'm your person, and I'll show up."

That's what we remember. That's what counts.

Not the daily greetings, or missed calls.

But that one hat.

Now, let me take you somewhere else entirely.

Chumki lived in a small town near the foothills of Meghalaya. She had always found her elder sister, Soniya, distant. Soniya had moved to Delhi for work years ago and rarely returned for festivals. Calls were brief. Texts were mechanical. For most of her teenage years, Chumki felt like Soniya had drifted out of their lives.

It bothered her.

She would often complain to her parents, "Why doesn't Didi ever ask how I'm doing? She doesn't care anymore."

Her parents would try to explain—"She's working hard, life is different there." But Chumki had anchored her understanding of Soniya on these absences.

Until one monsoon week, Chumki had a state-level debate championship she was preparing for. It was a big deal for her, the first time she was presenting something beyond her town.

To her surprise, Soniya called and asked if she could visit.

When she arrived, she didn't come empty-handed. She brought cue cards, trained Chumki on how to structure arguments, and stayed up nights rehearsing with her. For five full days, Soniya wore only one hat—the hat of a proud and loving sister.

On the morning of the event, she helped Chumki pin her badge, reviewed her notes one last time, and stood quietly at the back of the auditorium, smiling with tears in her eyes.

After the event, Soniya hugged her tightly and left that night to catch a flight back.

The calls became brief again. The texts were again sparse. But Chumki no longer judged her by that.

Because she had seen the one true hat.

And that was enough.

In the years that followed, every time Soniya failed to call during

Diwali, or forgot to reply to a long message, Chumki would smile and say, "But she came for my debate. That's who she is."

And in remembering that version, she found peace.

Sometimes, even in moments where we need someone the most, they don't show up.

They don't call. They don't come.

You wonder: where were they?

And it hurts. Deeply.

But their absence might not reflect their affection. It might reflect their reality.

Maybe their other hats were too loud—urgent responsibilities, personal crises, emotional overwhelm.

Or maybe they just didn't know how to be there.

Some people freeze in emotion. Some panic. Some withdraw.

It's not always easy to accept. But when we do, we find peace.

And that leads us to an important truth:

The way someone behaves with you when they wear one true hat tells you more about them than all the moments when they wore five at once.

Saurabh had a mentor in his early career, Mr. Mehra. Years passed. Saurabh moved cities, jobs, industries. Contact became sparse.

One evening, Saurabh spoke at a conference. When he looked out into the audience, he spotted a familiar face—Mr. Mehra, now retired, sitting in the third row.

After the talk, Saurabh approached him.

"Sir, you came all the way to Delhi?"

Mr. Mehra smiled. "Of course. I was your first fan."

No fanfare. No drama. Just a man, wearing one hat.

That's what it means to anchor your perception of people not in what they constantly do, but in who they are in those rare moments when everything else fades.

When their only job is being there for you.

So what do we do with this knowledge?

We shift our expectations.

We stop holding grudges based on everyday absences.

We start cherishing the people who have worn the true hat, even if only once. Because that moment was real.

We forgive the gaps between conversations.

We anchor ourselves in memory, not mood.

And most of all, we remember:

People are not just their bad days. They are not just their short replies. They are not just their distracted greetings.

They are the people who made you feel safe when it mattered. They are the people who laughed with you, encouraged you, stood beside you.

And that version—the one true hat—is the version worth remembering.

Can you remember a moment when someone wore just one hat for you?

Have you been that version for someone else recently?

Are there people in your life whose best selves you've forgotten because their present self is too busy?

Life doesn't always allow for consistency. But it does allow for truth.

And when you find the one true hat someone wears for you—hold on to it.

Because in a world full of shifting roles, that moment is the anchor.

And once you see someone wearing that hat, you never unsee it.

That is who they are.

That is who they have always been.

And that—if you choose to remember it—can be enough.

Pause and Reflect

- Can you remember a moment when someone set everything else aside just to be there for you?

- What made that version of them feel so real, so unforgettable?

- Have you ever shown up for someone else wearing only one hat—fully present, fully yours?

- Are there people you've unfairly judged by their distracted moments, while forgetting who they were in your defining ones?

- How would your relationships shift if you anchored your perception to someone's clearest moment, not their most scattered one?

Sometimes, one hat is enough. One moment is enough. The key is to see it, remember it, and let it guide how we hold space for each other.

CHAPTER SIX

WHEN THEY DON'T SHOW UP

*"Often it is not absence that wounds,
but the meaning we attach to it."*

Some chapters in life are not about what happened, but about what didn't.

You waited.

You reached out.

You hoped.

But... silence.

Sometimes, the deepest aches come not from harsh words or visible betrayal—but from absence.

And yet, this chapter is not about blame.

It's about understanding.

Let me begin with a story.

Apoorv had just moved back to India after nearly six years abroad. A lot had changed. His neighborhood was barely recognizable. His old friends were scattered across cities. But what hadn't changed was his longing to reconnect.

He texted his college best friend, Mehul.

"Back in town! Let's catch up?"

No reply.

A day passed. Then a week. Then a month.

Apoorv watched Mehul post stories of his new home, gym sessions, weekend brunches. Clearly, he wasn't missing. He just wasn't replying.

And it stung.

They had shared hostel rooms. Shared heartbreaks. Shared dreams.

Apoorv told himself: "Maybe he's changed."

Or worse: "Maybe he never cared."

Until, six months later, at a mutual friend's engagement, they met.

Mehul looked up, surprised—and emotional.

"I've been meaning to reply... I saw your message the day I came home to a family crisis. That week spiraled. And then I didn't know what to say... I didn't want to sound fake."

It wasn't malice.

It was life.

And fear.

And the inability to show up—not because he didn't care, but because he didn't know how.

You see, we all wear multiple hats. That much we've already explored.

But in some moments, despite the intensity of a situation, people still don't show up—even when they're wearing just one hat for you.

That's hard to accept.

We want to believe that the "true hat" always shows up.

But sometimes, that hat stays tucked away—not because the person doesn't love you, but because they're overwhelmed, uncertain, or unaware of how to be there.

Let's take a step back and break this down.

We often build silent expectations around how people should show up for us.

"If they really cared, they'd call."

"If I mattered, they'd be here."

But real life doesn't always cooperate with emotional math.

Sometimes, people don't show up because they're:

- Wearing a louder hat (parent to a sick child, manager in crisis mode, caregiver to aging parents)

- Emotionally frozen (they want to help but are paralyzed by uncertainty)

- Guilt-ridden (for being absent too long and not knowing how to return)

- Unaware (they genuinely didn't realize how much their presence mattered)

These are not excuses. They are realities.

Painful ones.

But understanding them can offer peace.

Niyati had just undergone surgery. A relatively minor one, but scary nonetheless. She kept waiting for a call from Simran, her childhood friend. The one who had once held her hand through her board exam anxiety. The one who had shown up to breakups with tubs of ice cream.

But this time—nothing.

A text. That too, three days later.

"Hey. Just heard. Hope you're okay."

Cold. Late. And unlike Simran.

Months later, when they finally spoke, Niyati asked why she hadn't called.

Simran broke down.

"I couldn't. I was scared. I had just lost someone to a surgery gone wrong, and... I froze. I didn't want to bring my fear into your space."

Sometimes, people stay silent because they think their presence might hurt more than help.

We often expect people to show up with the perfect words, the right gestures, the dramatic arrival.

But showing up isn't always cinematic.

Sometimes, showing up means sending a meal quietly, asking a mutual friend for updates, praying without saying a word.

And sometimes, showing up doesn't happen at all.

But even then—it doesn't mean they don't care.

They may simply not know how to be there.

Or they are already stretched thin by the other hats they're wearing.

Or—and this one is hard to admit—they are not equipped to deal with your vulnerability.

Let's be honest.

We've all been the one who didn't show up.

Missed a birthday because we were exhausted.

Didn't return a call because we didn't know what to say.
Drifted from a friend because our own life was heavy.

When we remember that, we begin to offer others the same forgiveness we secretly seek.

It's not about letting people off the hook.

It's about softening the edges of our assumptions.

Harsh had known Avni for over a decade. They had grown up in the same neighborhood, been on the same quiz team, laughed through teenage years.

Then life happened.

They drifted—different colleges, different cities, different schedules.

One day, Harsh heard from a mutual friend that Avni had gone through a really rough time—family issues, career setbacks, burnout.

He typed out a message: "Hey, I just heard. I hope you're okay. If you ever want to talk..."

But he didn't send it.

He read it again and felt it was too late, too awkward. Would she even want to hear from him now?

He deleted the message.

Years passed.

When they finally reconnected at a school reunion, Avni said, "There were days I kept hoping one of my old friends would reach out. I would've really appreciated it, no matter how long it had been."

Harsh smiled faintly. He had never sent that message—but he had thought of her. A lot.

Sometimes, we don't show up—not out of neglect, but hesitation.

And sometimes, that delay costs a little piece of connection we could've kept alive.

So what do we do when people don't show up?

We pause.

We examine the hats they might be wearing.

We ask ourselves: was this absence about me—or about them?

We remember the moments they did show up—and let that be the anchor.

Just like in Chapter 5, when someone wears the one true hat, we anchor onto it.

But when they don't wear it—when they disappear into their lives—we don't let that one absence overwrite the presence they once were.

And in that choice, we find peace.

If someone once showed up for you with their full self, that version still exists.

Don't let a season of silence convince you otherwise.

And if someone never did, maybe they didn't have the emotional tools.

Maybe they were wearing hats too heavy.

Or maybe, just maybe—they didn't know how to love you in the way you needed.

Even that truth can bring closure, if not comfort.

Pause and Reflect

- Who are the people you've held resentment towards for not showing up?

- Can you think of what hat they might have been wearing at that time?

- Have you ever stayed silent—not out of indifference, but fear or uncertainty?

- Can you forgive yourself for that? Can you forgive them?

When they don't show up, let it hurt—but also let it teach.

Don't rewrite their entire story.

Just recognize that one chapter was missing.

And maybe, someday, they'll return.

Wearing the right hat.

Ready to begin again.

CHAPTER SEVEN

THE GENTLE ART OF SEEING CLEARLY

*"We judge by shadows, forgetting
the sun that cast them."*

You've probably heard someone say, "People don't change." And maybe, you've heard the opposite just as often: "People change over time."

Both are true.

And neither is completely accurate.

The more important question is—what are you choosing to see in someone?

Let's begin with a story.

Kabir had just started working at a new office in Bengaluru. Fresh out of business school, enthusiastic and curious, he tried to befriend everyone. There was one person who caught his attention from day one—Anil, a mid-level manager, who always seemed polite but distant. He never joined lunch conversations, avoided small talk, and often seemed lost in thought.

Kabir, being the extrovert he was, tried initiating a few interactions. "Sir, great presentation today," or "Hey, we missed you at lunch."

Anil would nod, offer a smile, and move on.

Over time, Kabir heard murmurs—"He's arrogant," "Too full of himself," "Thinks he's above everyone."

Kabir didn't disagree.

One afternoon, Kabir forgot his lunch. Anil, who happened to be walking past, paused and said, "I brought extra. Want to share?"

Kabir was surprised. He hesitated, then nodded.

Over lunch, Anil opened up in fragments. He was mentoring his nephew for board exams at night, preparing a team to meet a critical deadline, and had recently started therapy to manage chronic stress. The weight he carried wasn't visible—but it was very real.

That one lunch changed Kabir's entire perspective.

Anil hadn't changed. Kabir had simply seen him clearly for the first time.

When people disappoint us, it's usually not because they did something objectively terrible—it's because they failed to behave the way we expected them to.

Expectations are tricky.

They're often formed from limited data: a few interactions,

secondhand stories, an impulsive judgment.

So when people don't match the version we've constructed in our minds, we react—not to them, but to the shadow of what we expected.

We stop seeing them. We only see the mismatch.

And yet, every person is far more layered than we give them credit for.

Varun had a college friend, Ajay, who almost never stayed in touch—until he needed something. A reference. A contact. A document. A favor.

Every time Varun saw Ajay's name flash on his phone, he'd sigh. "Wonder what he wants this time."

To him, Ajay had become that person—the one who showed up only when it was convenient, or when he needed help.

Over time, Varun started distancing himself. Ignoring calls. Taking longer to reply.

At a college reunion, Ajay caught up with him over chai. After some small talk, he said, "I know I haven't stayed in touch the way I should've. You probably think I only call when I need something."

Varun offered a careful smile.

Ajay continued, "It's just that I know you always have my back. That's why I reach out to you. You're one of the few people I can still count on."

They moved on to other conversations. The evening passed with laughter, photos, and nostalgia.

Later that night, Varun overheard another friend talking about Ajay.

"Man, that guy has too much on his plate. Did you know he's leading a team through layoffs, and doing a night course to upskill? On top of that, he's mentoring kids on weekends and handling some ugly legal issue in the family. And a long-distance relationship, too."

Varun was quiet.

Ajay hadn't made excuses. He hadn't offloaded his story. But the puzzle pieces clicked.

Ajay wasn't reaching out only when he wanted. He was reaching out when he could. When his other hats gave him just enough space.

And he wasn't reaching out to everyone.

He was reaching out to Varun, because he trusted him.

Ajay hadn't changed.

Varun had just seen him clearly.

That night, when Varun drove home, he scrolled through their old messages. And a curious warmth filled him.

Not guilt. Not obligation.

Just understanding.

On a rainy Thursday, Tara stood at a crowded bus stop. Next to her, an elderly man held a dripping file folder close to his chest. He looked agitated. When the bus arrived, he jostled past her, bumping into her shoulder.

Tara muttered under her breath, annoyed.

Minutes later, she saw him again—standing inside the bus, speaking softly to the conductor. She overheard him say, "My daughter's visa application... these are the last documents. Had to leave the hospital to get them."

Suddenly, everything made sense.

That man hadn't been rude.

He'd been desperate.

She had only seen the shove. Not the story behind it.

It takes effort to pause and consider that maybe—

Someone's coldness is actually shyness.

Someone's delay is driven by guilt, not disrespect.

Someone's silence is shielding you from their own chaos.

Someone's flakiness is their survival mechanism, not indifference.

Seeing clearly doesn't mean excusing all behavior.

It simply means interpreting it with a wider lens.

One that allows for context.

One that allows for humanity.

Shruti worked as an operations lead in a startup. Her team included Tanmay, a shy but sincere guy who rarely spoke unless spoken to. He always brought his own lunch, never joined team outings, and usually sat alone.

At first, Shruti assumed he didn't want to engage.

Then one afternoon, the team's food delivery got delayed, and everyone was hungry and irritable. Shruti casually said, "Tanmay, your lunch always smells so good. What's the secret?"

Tanmay hesitated, then smiled and said, "It's my grandmother. She insists on packing my lunch herself every morning."

Everyone laughed. The moment was warm. Shruti asked more.

Turned out, Tanmay was caring for his grandparents, the only family he had left. His introversion wasn't aloofness. It was quiet exhaustion mixed with deep responsibility.

From that day, Shruti started inviting him more warmly. And Tanmay slowly opened up.

Nothing dramatic happened. Just a small shift.

But it made all the difference.

By now, you already know about hats—the roles people wear and how their behavior is a result of which hat dominates at any given moment.

When someone fails to show up, or disappoints you in their everyday behavior, it's easy to label them: "He's so selfish," "She's never there for me," "They don't care."

But if we look closer, we realize their behavior wasn't personal.

It was just the louder hat talking.

In Chapter 6, we explored how some people simply don't show up—not because they don't care, but because they don't know how to.

In this chapter, we take that one step further.

We don't just forgive people for what they failed to do.

We actively choose to see what they did do—even if it wasn't perfect.

That's what clarity is.

Not emotional fog.

But emotional sharpness.

Once you truly see someone—their struggles, their efforts, their quieter acts of care—you can love them more honestly.

Not with less heart.

But with less fear.

You stop over-interpreting their mistakes.

You stop weaponizing their silences.

You begin to love people in ways that are real, grounded, sustainable.

Love becomes less about transaction, and more about recognition.

Yes, sometimes, seeing clearly does hurt.

Sometimes, you realize that the person you hoped would change, won't.

Or that their truest self is too different from who you are.

Even then, clarity is a gift.

Because it allows you to choose.

To let go, or hold on—knowing what you're choosing.

That's far better than clinging to a version that never existed.

Can you remember a time when you misunderstood someone's intentions?

Is there someone who's misunderstood you?

Have you taken time to see someone's quieter efforts lately?

Have you offered yourself the same clarity you offer others?

We live in a world obsessed with being seen.

But the real magic?

Is in seeing others.

Fully.

Patiently.

Pause and Reflect

- Have you ever mistaken silence for arrogance, or busyness for neglect?

- What if the version of someone you carry is only a silhouette—missing the light behind it?

- Who might surprise you, if you chose to look again?

- Is there someone you've written off... not because of who they are, but when you saw them?

- And within your own story—how many times have you longed to be seen fully, beyond the moment you were caught in?

Sometimes, clarity isn't about being right.

It's about being willing to look again—softly, and with more light.

Seeing clearly isn't about perfection. It's about choosing curiosity over conclusion.

THE ANCHOR WITHIN

*"Some bonds fade with time,
others remain— not in memory, but in meaning."*

Have you ever wondered why some bonds feel so unshakeable?

Even after months or years of no contact, no messages, no visits—you meet someone and it feels as if nothing has changed. The familiarity, the comfort, the shorthand language you speak without words. It all just returns.

That's not an accident. That's the magic of anchoring.

Aditi and Nikhil had been childhood friends in Indore. They lived two buildings apart and spent endless afternoons flying kites, sharing homework hacks, and exchanging secrets under the staircase.

Then life happened. Different cities. Different careers. Different timelines.

They kept in touch for a few years, then slowly drifted. Birthdays turned to texts. Texts turned to silence.

Almost a decade later, Aditi returned to Indore for a cousin's wedding. On a whim, she messaged Nikhil.

"Still in town?"

He was. They met that evening on their old rooftop.

At first, there was the usual small talk. Work. Life. Cities. Weather.

But within minutes, the walls fell away.

They were back to their rhythm. Joking about the same neighbors. Remembering old fights. Laughing at how they once believed chewing gum could stick broken things back together.

It was as if time had never passed.

What made that possible?

It wasn't memory. It wasn't nostalgia.

It was the anchor Aditi had always carried for Nikhil.

An anchor, in the emotional sense, is the version of someone you choose to hold on to. The version that felt the most true, the most safe, the most them.

It usually gets formed in moments of authenticity—during a vulnerable conversation, a shared crisis, an unfiltered celebration. When someone shows up wearing only one hat.

No distractions. No pretenses. Just presence.

That's the moment your heart takes a snapshot. And that version of them—that one hat moment—gets embedded deep within you.

Even as time and life layer on more complexities, your memory of them remains steady.

That's your anchor.

Samar was stuck in traffic on Diwali evening, alone in his car, watching fireworks light up the sky. His wife and kids were visiting her parents. His friends were out of town. The city felt festive but distant.

He thought of Mehul, his childhood neighbor and once-best friend. They hadn't spoken in six years. Not after a bitter misunderstanding involving borrowed money and bruised pride.

Samar didn't even remember the full details anymore. But he remembered something else.

The time Mehul had stayed by his side all night when his father was hospitalized.

The time Mehul missed his own engagement pre-function just to help Samar fix a broken car en route to a job interview.

Those weren't small things. That was the real Mehul.

The anchor held strong.

Samar dialed the number.

"Hello?"

"Hey," Samar said. "Happy Diwali. I don't know why it took me this long."

There was a pause. Then a quiet laugh.

"Took you long enough," Mehul replied. "Come over. Maa made too many laddoos."

Sometimes, we let pride and silence build walls around bonds that still matter. We carry the burden of a moment, and forget the weight of a history.

But anchoring allows us to remember the version of someone that once made us feel safe and seen.

Samar didn't just reach out to Mehul because it was Diwali. He reached out because the anchor was still intact. And Mehul responded not from the place of a grudge, but from the same version of himself Samar remembered.

That's the quiet strength of emotional anchoring—it helps us reconnect when words and time have long failed.

Riya worked with Tanay for over three years in the same tech firm. He was smart, energetic, always willing to help. During one particularly difficult quarter, when she was overwhelmed with deadlines and personal stress, Tanay silently picked up her slack. No questions. No drama.

She never forgot that.

Then Tanay left for another company. Riya congratulated him, but their chats quickly faded.

Years later, she heard he had started a startup. She messaged him to say hi—and didn't hear back.

A month passed. Two. It stung.

"Maybe he was never really that kind," she thought. "Maybe it was just convenient back then."

But that thought didn't sit well.

Because she remembered his eyes when she broke down at her desk.

She remembered how he stayed late without saying a word.

That wasn't convenience. That was character.

And she realized—Tanay might be wearing too many hats now. CEO. Fundraiser. Product Manager. Leader. Son. Partner.

But the anchor version of him—the friend in a storm—was real.

And she decided to hold on to that.

An anchor isn't an excuse for someone's toxic behavior.

It's not a reason to tolerate being hurt, ignored, or manipulated.

But in most relationships that matter, our disappointments aren't because people have changed entirely. They're because we forget their layers.

We judge someone based on the current hat they're wearing—when once, we saw them clearly.

Anchors are reminders. Not illusions.

Take a moment and think of three people you've grown distant from.

Ask yourself:

When did I see them at their best?

What hat were they wearing then?

Did they ever show up fully, just for me?

What if that's still who they are deep down?

Now ask:

Who might be holding my anchor too?

Have I allowed noise and distance to make me forget who I am to them?

These answers don't have to lead to action. Sometimes, clarity is enough.

In a small town in Assam, Devika ran a bakery that had once been her father's. She grew up learning how to fold butter into dough, how to take cash without a calculator, and how to remember everyone's birthday order.

One regular customer, Mr. Roy, had moved away years ago. He used to come every Sunday morning to buy a dozen nankhatai biscuits and chat about politics, cricket, and life.

Then he stopped. Moved to Kolkata. Time moved on.

One afternoon, she received a letter. Just a simple envelope with an old stamp and shaky handwriting.

"Dear Devika, I saw a pack of nankhatai in a store here today, and thought of you. They weren't as good. They never will be. Thank you for being a bright spot in my Sundays. You probably don't remember me much, but I remember you well. I hope you're still baking."

Devika sat on the bakery steps and smiled.

Anchors work both ways.

We are not the only ones carrying emotional anchors.

Sometimes, others have held on to a version of us too—a version we might have even forgotten. A moment when we were kind without knowing, present without realizing, important without effort.

The bakery letter wasn't about biscuits—it was about memory, about warmth, about acknowledgment. And it was proof that even in the smallest gestures, we leave behind anchors for others to hold on to.

We all have people we've misread. Misjudged. Misremembered.

And we all have people we've loved fiercely in quiet moments.

What if we learned to trust those moments more than the mood of the present?

What if we built relationships not just on proximity, but on clarity?

What if we stopped expecting people to always behave like their best version, and instead... just remembered it ourselves?

That's what an anchor is for.

To help you hold on to the version of someone that mattered the most.

The one that gave you hope.

The one that showed you love.

The one that reminded you of your own capacity to feel.

Because that version still exists.

Behind the noise. Beneath the hats.

And maybe, just maybe, they're holding on to your anchor too.

Pause and Reflect

- Are you anchoring to someone's best version—or their latest behavior?

- Think of someone you've grown apart from. What's the one moment that still makes you smile?

- If someone remembers you, what memory do you hope they've kept?

- Are there moments when you, too, showed up as your truest self—quiet, present, undistracted?

- Have you been holding someone at a distance for who they became... instead of who they once were for you?

- And if a version of you lives on in someone's heart—are you proud of the version they remember?

You don't have to speak every day to still belong to each other.

You don't need constant proof to trust what was once unmistakable.

Some people are not part of your routine.

They're part of your foundation.

Remember that.

Let it guide how gently you judge, and how deeply you care.

Bringing It All Together

Chapter 1 reminded us of a time when relationships felt simpler—when roles were fewer, and presence meant something whole. It invited us to reflect on how life's pace, responsibilities, and distractions fragment our connections over time, making the familiar feel strangely distant. It laid the emotional foundation for everything that followed, urging us to remember how much clarity we once shared with those who mattered.

Chapter 2 explored how, over time, we begin wearing multiple hats—shifting roles that influence how we speak, listen, and show up. It offered the insight that our misunderstandings often stem not from a change in who someone is, but from the increasing complexity of who they have to be. It asked us to look beyond the surface and see that the person we once knew still exists—just buried under layers of responsibility and change.

Chapter 3 reframed emotional drift as a by-product of these accumulating hats. It showed how even the people we feel closest to can begin to feel unfamiliar—not because they've changed entirely, but because we've both evolved into versions that no longer recognize the old rhythm. This chapter nudged us to reflect on how the disconnects we feel are often not intentional—but circumstantial.

Chapter 4 shed light on the fragile nature of communication. It showed us that the words we hear are filtered through the hats we wear—and that misunderstandings arise when interpretation overtakes intention. It urged us to pause before reacting, to ask what lens the other person might be wearing, and to offer more grace in our everyday conversations.

Chapter 5 was the emotional heart of the book—the moment of deep reveal. It introduced us to the idea of the one true hat: the version of someone that shows up for us in their purest form, even if only once. It taught us that anchoring our relationships to that version—the one we saw in a moment of presence, vulnerability, or care—can keep us from letting temporary roles cloud a lifetime of connection.

Chapter 6 addressed a more difficult reality—when people don't show up at all. It moved us from disappointment to understanding by unpacking the reasons behind emotional absence: fear, overwhelm, timing, or emotional unreadiness. It also turned the mirror back on us, asking when we have failed to show up, and how empathy begins with acknowledging both sides of silence.

Chapter 7 deepened our perspective further by showing that what we often interpret as indifference may just be someone surviving their own chaos. It reminded us that judgment is often a reaction to shadows—projections of what we expected, not what was real. When we choose to see clearly, we shift from disappointment to understanding, from resentment to compassion.

Chapter 8 offered closure and hope. It introduced us to the idea of anchors—emotional snapshots of someone's best self that we carry forward, even when they're no longer near. It reminded us that others carry anchors of us, too. And that while people may drift, what was once real can always be remembered—and sometimes, rediscovered.

Together, these chapters form a map. Not of perfection, but of understanding. Not of fixing people, but of seeing them—fully, gently, and without assumption.

Because when our hats don't match, it's not the end of the bond.

It's simply the beginning of a new kind of awareness.

And from there, we find our way back.

Final Thoughts

If you've made it this far, thank you. Not just for reading, but for staying open.

Somewhere along the way, maybe you thought of someone.
Someone you've misjudged. Someone you've missed.
Someone who wore a different hat than the one you needed them to wear.

Maybe you saw your own reflection too. The times you disappeared. The times you showed up. The hats you forgot you were wearing.

That's all this book ever hoped to do.
Not to give you advice. Not to hand out lessons.
But to offer a mirror. A lens. A little space to pause and see again.

Because once you see people clearly,
You stop resenting their absence.
You stop over-reading their silence.
You start remembering who they were—when they were just *yours*.

That version is still inside them.
Still inside you.
Waiting to be seen again.

So go back.
To the person.
To the memory.
To the connection you thought was lost.

Chances are—it was never lost. Just covered by a hat.